THE NATURE OF HOPE

"For I know the plans that I have for you," declares the LORD,

"plans for welfare and not for calamity to give you a future and a hope."

JEREMIAH 29:11

Broadman & Holman Publishers
Nashville, Tennessee
www.broadmanholman.com

Printed in Belgium
ISBN 0-8054-2700-7

$\mathcal{D}$EDICATIONS

To John C. Cameron,

mentor, friend, and great Christian

who understands the nature of hope.

—Adrian Rogers

To my beloved mother, Wilma Fox,

whose unconditional love was a reflection

of the hope and grace of God.

—Tom Fox

THE 𝒫ROMISE OF HOPE

THE 𝒫ROVISION OF HOPE

THE 𝒫ERSON OF HOPE

FOREWORD

Did you know that nature has its own personal Scripture verse? Romans 8:19 tells us: "The creation waits in eager expectation for the sons of God to be revealed." The J.B. Phillips Translation renders it like this: "The whole creation is on tiptoe to see the wonderful sight of the sons of God coming into their own."

On tiptoe. . . .

Yes, in some mysterious way, the flowers, plants, and animals—the seascapes and landscapes—all wait in eager expectation for a glory yet to be revealed.

As you turn the pages of *The Nature of Hope*, as you ponder the thoughts of my friend, Dr. Adrian Rogers, and relish the stunning nature photography of Dr. Tom Fox, it's my prayer that you'll consider this: If the creation has this kind of an earnest expectation, surely we believers should have nothing less! If the whole inanimate creation is eagerly looking forward to the appearing of Jesus, this same hope—even a brighter hope—should grip our hearts and minds.

How is the nature of your hope today? Do you find yourself looking forward to the glorious appearing of our Savior? You and I need not wait for Him in a dull sort of way with a ho-hum attitude. We can rejoice in our hope. We can yearn and fervently anticipate all that Jesus has in store for us.

Friend, I'm asking you to take a hint from the photos and the devotionals on the following pages, because we can learn a thing or two from creation. As you muse over these images of God's glorious handiwork, think about Romans 8:19.

After all, if nature waits on tiptoe for the coming of Jesus, you and I shouldn't be caught flat-footed. May your anticipation be truly happy and eager.

That is the nature of hope.

—*Joni Eareckson Tada*

Summer 2003

THE
$\mathcal{P}$ROMISE
OF HOPE

Hope will endure trials, conquer temptations, and enjoy heaven below.

—CHARLES HADDON SPURGEON

Charles Haddon Spurgeon has always been one of my favorite preachers. In a sermon entitled "The Hope of Future Bliss," he challenged, "Have you ever gone to the great Niagara of hope, and drunk the spray with ravishing delight; for the very spray of heaven is glory to one's soul!"

This promise of divine hope truly quenches our thirst in the wilderness of trials and temptations. "For thou art my hope, O Lord GOD: thou art my trust from my youth" (Psalm 71:5).

Our hope, our trust, our confidence is anchored in the constant activity of God. He graces us with His promises, guards us with His presence, guides us with His principles, and gladdens us with His provisions. Surely, this is heaven on earth . . . and the promise of hope eternal.

CANYONLANDS NATIONAL PARK, UTAH

lovingkindness

FIRST LIGHT

The Lord's lovingkindnesses indeed never cease, for His compassions never fail. They are new every morning; great is Thy faithfulness. "The Lord is my portion," says my soul, "therefore I have hope in Him."

—LAMENTATIONS 3:22-24

It has been wisely said, "Every morning lean thine arms awhile upon the windowsill of heaven and gaze upon the Lord. Then, with this vision in thy heart, turn strong to meet the day."

The sky was full of storms as Tom was retiring for sleep the night before taking this picture. But he awoke the next morning to an amazing dawn. Have you ever gone to bed with the storms of life beating upon your heart's windowsill? Let me give you a promise of hope: God's compassions never cease. They are new every morning.

This book is your opportunity to experience this truth afresh. So come away, my friend. The Creator of the universe is waiting for you. Retreat from the world's urgent pleas and enter into the quietness of His presence. Great is His faithfulness. Indeed, this is the promise of hope.

Great Smoky Mountains National Park, Tennessee

NEVER ALONE

For He Himself has said, "I will never leave you nor forsake you."

—HEBREWS 13:5

Greek scholars say that this promise from the book of Hebrews actually consists of five negatives. It literally says that God will *never, no not ever, no never* forsake you.

Perhaps your husband or wife has left you. Perhaps at some point in your life, a parent walked out on you, leaving you uncared for and unwanted. But my precious brother or sister in Christ, God has promised to never abandon you. Though you may feel as alone as this tree in the middle of the Colorado Plateau, His promise of hope is certain for you.

Just as this tree is not only growing but thriving in the midst of a rocky, barren place, you too can be assured that "He who began a good work in you will perfect it until the day of Christ Jesus" (Philippians 1:6). He is here, and He is not leaving. You are never alone.

COLORADO PLATEAU

THROUGH THE WATERS

When you pass through the waters, I will be with you; and through the rivers, they will not overflow you.

—ISAIAH 43:2

The Spanish have a proverb: "There is no home without its hush." There is no place, however safe and secure, where the troubles of life cannot threaten to silence the hum and laughter of daily living.

But God has promised His children that in Him—and Him alone—is safe passage through the storm. Our loving Father offers us more than a faith that sparkles when the sun is shining. He daily makes available to us a faith that transforms raging waters into pure displays of His glory and grace.

In 1891, Maxwell Cornelius wrote: "Not now, but in the coming years / It may be in the better land / We'll read the meaning of our tears / And there, some time, we'll understand." You may be going through deep water right now. But though you must pass through the rivers, you will not drown. Fear not, for God is with you.

ZION NATIONAL PARK, UTAH

DISPELLING THE *D*ARKNESS

*T*he LORD *my God will enlighten my darkness.*

—PSALM 18:28

Have you ever been through the dark patches of life and found it hard to see your way? Perhaps at the time, nothing seemed to make sense. Maybe it was a wayward child, a financial reversal, a sudden tragedy, or a broken relationship. You tried reading the Bible and praying, yet the darkness persisted, relentless.

Often those who have had the greatest devotion have known the deepest darkness. Think of Job, Habakkuk, David, Paul, John the Baptist. Faith can be born in the light, but many times it is developed in the dark. As Thomas Watson said, "Where reason cannot wade, faith must swim."

Do you want your darkness swept away? Or at least a ray of light to lead you through it? Then look to the Lord. Lean on His promise of hope. There are treasures in the darkness that only God can help you discover.

WIND RIVER RANGE, WYOMING

$\mathscr{S}$HELTERED

$\mathscr{A}$nd [He] will be like a refuge from the wind, and a shelter from the storm . . . like the shade of a huge rock.

—ISAIAH 32:2

 The purple phacelia in Tom's photograph gets its name from the Greek word *phakelos*, meaning "cluster." If you'll look closely, you'll see that their flowering spikes do indeed grow that way.

I find this quite interesting in the context of this verse from Isaiah. The prophet promises that God will be our refuge and shelter against the storms of life. But many times, God provides this comfort as we surround ourselves with other believers, drawing strength through the shared love and concern of others. For like Jesus said, "Where two or three come together in my name, there am I with them" (Matthew 18:20)—in clusters of caring and compassion.

When we go through hard times, we receive help not only from God's Word but also from God's people. The Rock that protects us during the torrential winds of suffering multiplies our comfort through the blessing of Christian friends and family.

GREAT SMOKY MOUNTAINS NATIONAL PARK, TENNESSEE

IN THE CLEFT OF THE ROCK

I *will put you in the cleft of the rock and cover you with My hand.*

—EXODUS 33:22

 In Exodus 33, we read that Moses asked God, "Show me Thy glory" (v. 18). I wonder if he knew what he was asking—the Almighty Creator of heaven and earth revealing His holiness to man.

Yet even more astounding was that God agreed to comply to this incredible request. And when the glory of the Lord passed by, "Moses made haste, and bowed his head toward the earth, and worshipped" (Exodus 34:8).

Friend, God's presence is real. Call on Him, for He is there—able to meet your deepest needs, even when your way seems hemmed in by the immovable rocks of impossibility. As the great hymn writer Fanny Crosby wrote, "He hideth my soul in the cleft of the rock / That shadows a dry, thirsty land / He hideth my life in the depths of His love / And covers me there with His hand."

COLORADO PLATEAU

WONDERS ON EARTH

And I will display wonders in the sky and on the earth . . . and it will come about that whoever calls on the name of the LORD will be delivered.

—JOEL 2:30, 32

One of my favorite verses in all the Bible is Acts 2:21: "And it shall come to pass, that whosoever shall call on the name of the Lord shall be saved."

Do you know why I like this verse so much? Because like these passages from the book of Joel, it conveys a rock-solid promise of deliverance. The conclusion I draw from it is not that I *might* be saved but that I *shall* be saved. Both of these statements from the Word of God declare the blessed assurance that whoever calls on the name of the Lord *will* be delivered!

Lewis Jones expressed this same confidence in a hymn he wrote in 1899, and it still rings true today: "There is power, power, wonder-working power / In the precious blood of the Lamb." Do you need His deliverance today? You can have it—just by calling on His powerful name.

GRAND CANYON NATIONAL PARK, ARIZONA

WITHSTANDING THE *Storms*

In the world you have tribulation, but take courage; I have overcome the world.

—JOHN 16:33

 What do you do when troubles descend upon you like a raging storm? The Bible tells us to stand firm (like this tree in the Smoky Mountains) because God is at work, developing patience and perseverance in us, allowing us to experience His strength.

Bible scholar William Barclay said, "This is not the patience that can sit down and bow its head and let things descend upon it, passively enduring it until the storm has passed; it is the spirit which can bear things not simply with resignation but with blazing hope. It is not a patience which grimly waits for the end, but a patience which radiantly hopes for the dawn."

One of the greatest marks of your faith and confidence in the Almighty is your perseverance when trouble comes, your unwillingness to surrender your steadfast hope in His perfect will. Let the winds blow; your anchor holds.

GREAT SMOKY MOUNTAINS NATIONAL PARK, TENNESSEE

LOOK TO THE *R*OCK

*L*isten to me, you who pursue righteousness, who seek the LORD:

look to the rock from which you were hewn. . . .

I, even I, am He who comforts you.

—ISAIAH 51:1,12

I want you to notice in this picture how everything—from the clouds in the sky to the swirling lines of stone—all seem to be focusing your eye on the pinnacle of this intriguing rock formation.

This is what God can do in our lives every day, even when we feel overwhelmed by worry and overpowered by our problems. He can help us focus our attention on the source of our comfort—our Savior, our Rock!

Paul knew this. That's why when he spoke of his ordeals in ministry, he could say, "We are troubled on every side, yet not distressed; we are perplexed, but not in despair; Persecuted, but not forsaken; cast down, but not destroyed" (2 Corinthians 4:8-9). Paul could wake up refreshed each morning because he knew his unchanging, immovable God was in control.

And in this, we can all take comfort.

COLORADO PLATEAU

GREAT AND MIGHTY THINGS

Call to Me, and I will answer you, and I will tell you great and mighty things, which you do not know.

—JEREMIAH 33:3

Have you ever seen a more glorious dawn? Probably not—because Tom had to rise early in the morning and brave minus 25° temperatures to capture these spectacular morning hues.

Are you willing to get up early enough in the morning for God to show you "great and mighty things"? Dear friend, I cannot stress enough the importance of getting alone with God every day. Psalm 91:15 says, in speaking of the believer, "He shall call upon Me, and I will answer him: I will be with him in trouble; I will deliver him, and honor him."

What are you praying for today? Do you believe God can answer? Do you believe He *will* answer? Then come with anticipation and an eager heart to the throne of grace. When you do, He has promised to show you "great and mighty things."

GRAND TETON NATIONAL PARK, WYOMING

A LIGHT IN THE DARKNESS

And if you give yourself to the hungry, and satisfy the desire of the afflicted,
then your light will rise in darkness, and your gloom will become like midday.

—ISAIAH 58:10

 Jesus said you are to "let your light so shine before men, that they may see your good works, and glorify your Father which is in heaven" (Matthew 5:16). You say, "But I'm not much, Brother Rogers. I can't sing. I can't teach. What kind of difference could I make?"

A world of difference! Because, guess what? Jesus isn't telling you to shine *your* light; He wants you to shine *His* light. And He can do that through anyone!

Perhaps your light is not very flashy. But tell me, which light is most important: a crystal chandelier that decorates the foyer, or that single bulb that keeps you from falling down the basement steps? Obedience, not ornamentation, is what's important. So let Christ shine His light through you. You will not only drive the darkness out of your *own* heart, but you will shine His hope into another's.

ARCHES NATIONAL PARK, UTAH

IN A DRY AND WEARY LAND

Blessed are those who hunger and thirst for righteousness, for they shall be satisfied.

—MATTHEW 5:6

The Grand Canyon can be a forbidding place of great hunger and thirst. Yet if you look hard enough (as Tom does when he is scouting for great photo opportunities), you can discover God's serendipities of life, such as this bouquet of yellow wildflowers growing amidst the barren landscape. What a sign of hope!

Do you feel as though you're in a dry and weary land today? Hungry for a better life, a deeper calm, a more fulfilling existence? That hidden hunger can only be satisfied by Jesus Christ. You may not know it; you may not understand it; you may not even agree with it. But it is true: the deepest need of your life is a right relationship with God through the Lord Jesus Christ. Only in fellowship with Him are you guaranteed satisfaction.

GRAND CANYON NATIONAL PARK, ARIZONA

A SOUL IN *D*ROUGHT

*T*he LORD *will guide you continually, and satisfy your soul in drought. . . . You shall be like a watered garden, and like a spring of water, whose waters do not fail.*

—ISAIAH 58:11

A stream in the desert is rare, so when Tom set out on his thirty-mile hike into the Grand Canyon, he didn't go unprepared. He studied his route ahead of time, and he brought along a map which led him to a spring where he could replenish his water supply. The spring in this picture is where he camped that day.

Oh, that every person would not only consult God's Word but would obediently follow it. You don't have to wander aimlessly looking for satisfaction in life. In Christ you can find healing waters of refreshing forgiveness, restoring grace, and replenishing peace.

For God promises, "In the wilderness shall waters break out, and streams in the desert. And the parched ground shall become a pool, and the thirsty land springs of water" (Isaiah 35:6-7).

GRAND CANYON NATIONAL PARK, ARIZONA

ON $\mathscr{H}$IGH

The LORD *longs to be gracious to you, and therefore He waits on high to have compassion on you. . . . How blessed are all those who long for Him.*

—ISAIAH 30:18

 I thought of one of my daughter's poems when I saw this beautiful springtime display of wildflowers in a mountain's courtyard.

Speaking of our Lord Jesus, she wrote, "He dries all my tears / Calms every storm and He conquers my fears / He gives me hinds' feet to walk on high places / He floods my soul with His heavenly graces / When I am weak, then His strength makes me strong . . . / When the doubt comes, I'll lift up my eyes to my Savior above / And Jesus will make me glad."

I never cease to be amazed that the glorious Most High God longs to be gracious to me, that he desires to have an intimate relationship with me. Each time I look up to Him, He graciously descends to commune with me. Glory to God!

WIND RIVER RANGE, WYOMING

POURED OUT

"Test Me now in this," says the LORD of hosts, "if I will not open for you the windows of heaven, and pour out for you a blessing until it overflows."

—MALACHI 3:10

The Almighty King of kings wants to open the windows of heaven and shower you with blessings! How does that make you feel?

Perhaps you feel like many others, that you have sinned so terribly that God would never bless you. Friend, you couldn't be more wrong. The Bible is resplendent with promises of His love (Romans 8:31-39, Titus 3:4-7, 1 John 3:1-3). There's no sin you can commit that will make God stop loving you. His arms are wide open. Will you test Him now in this?

Get near to the heart of God, turn over to Him all your doubts and fears, then get ready for a blessing. For just as the waters pour over these rocks in the New England forest, God wants to pour over you with His love.

WHITE MOUNTAINS, NEW HAMPSHIRE

ℋEAVEN

Your sun will set no more, neither will your moon wane; for you will have the
LORD for an everlasting light, and the days of your mourning will be finished.

—ISAIAH 60:20

Heaven is a place where there will be no more
suffering, no more sickness, and no more sin.
Surely it will be more glorious than anything we
have ever known. Words fail me as I try to conceive of the sacred secrets that heaven will tell,
the beauty that heaven will display, the joy that heaven will hold.

But more than these things, I long for something more. As Fanny Crosby wrote, "Through
the gates to the city / In a robe of spotless white / He will lead me where no tears will ever fall /
In the glad song of the ages / I shall mingle with delight / But I long to meet my Savior first of all."

What greater hope can we have than to know that we will see our Savior face to face?
Heaven awaits us—the redeemed. And even more does He—our Redeemer!

GREAT SMOKY MOUNTAINS NATIONAL PARK, TENNESSEE

THE
$\mathscr{P}$ROVISION
OF HOPE

It was the season of light. It was the spring of hope.

—CHARLES DICKENS

Spring is a time of renewal and rejoicing over God's promises, a fresh reminder of His continuing commitment to replenish the earth with new life. In winter we wonder; in spring we know.

I think of that simple line from the childhood song, "Jesus loves me, this I know." Yes, dear friend, hope is more than just wishful thinking. We can know it. It is a bedrock assurance, mingled with the anticipation that God is here for us.

You may feel as alone as this purple flower, yet this flower is the color of royalty—just as you are. For as First Peter 2:9 promises, "Ye are a chosen generation, a royal priesthood, an holy nation, a peculiar people; that ye should show forth the praises of Him who hath called you out of darkness into His marvelous light." God is for you. He is your provision of hope.

GREAT SMOKY MOUNTAINS NATIONAL PARK, TENNESSEE

WONDERFULLY MADE

I will give thanks to Thee, for I am fearfully and wonderfully made; wonderful are Thy works.

—PSALM 139:14

 Have you ever seen a geyser this beautiful? It is truly a phenomenal sight. But I know a more wonderful sight. When was the last time you looked in a mirror? Now, that is a beautiful sight—more glorious than any geyser, more miraculous than any mammal, more intriguing than any insect! You think this geyser is incredible? You are a rare and precious jewel!

God never makes duplicates, only originals. And because you are the handiwork of Almighty God, you are special. You are one of a kind. In fact, if you had been the only soul that ever lived on this earth, Jesus Christ would still have loved you enough to die for you.

Now, take a look in the mirror again . . . and see a wondrous work of God!

GREAT BASIN, NEVADA

ANGELS *Unseen*

The angel of the L<small>ORD</small> *encamps around those who fear Him, and rescues them.*

—P<small>SALM</small> 34:7

Just before this photograph was taken, a thunderstorm had driven Tom and his friends into their tents for refuge. As the storm abated, however, Tom ventured out to see if he could catch a glimpse of the setting sun. What he saw instead was as a "fire in the sky," like the glory of God.

How often we are unaware of God's guardian angels in the storms of life. Psalm 68:17 says, "The chariots of God are twenty thousand, even thousands of angels: the Lord is among them, as in Sinai, in the holy place."

When you are in the midst of a storm, ask the Lord to open your eyes and help you see His presence, right there with you. God protects His own. No harm can approach you without having to pass through God's angels first.

WIND RIVER RANGE, WYOMING

SANDSTONE SYMPHONY

He brought me up out of the pit . . . and He put a new song in my mouth.

—PSALM 40:2-3

Hope is not dependent upon your circumstances. Does that sound hard and calloused? You may be sick, even in the hospital. You may have just lost your job. You may be dealing with a loss more devastating than any you've ever experienced. Yet you can still have hope. How?

The fortieth Psalm holds the key. In verses 1 and 2, we learn that David waited upon God. And God not only saved him, but He also set David's feet upon a rock, gave him direction for his life, and . . . what? . . . put a song in his heart.

The next time you are tempted to sit down for a pity party with the devil, invite God Almighty into the room by singing praises to His name! God wants to dress you in His royal robes of hope. He invites you now. Will you allow Him?

SLOT CANYON, ARIZONA

RIVERS IN THE *DESERT*

I have given waters in the wilderness and rivers in the desert, to give drink to My chosen people.

—ISAIAH 43:20

Thunder Falls seems to mysteriously emerge from a cave in the Grand Canyon. And yet, from God's perspective, He knows from whence the water comes, and He has channeled it in precisely this path to give life-giving sustenance to His creation.

Nothing is beyond God's control. He can create rivers in the desert—or even deserts in a river!—as He did when He parted the Red Sea for the Israelites.

Trust me: you can know the hope of God. There is not a movement He does not see, a motive He does not know, or a murmur He does not hear. Neither darkness, distance, nor death can hide you from His love. He knows where you are and how to care for you. Call on Him today . . . wherever you are.

GRAND CANYON NATIONAL PARK, ARIZONA

A STRONG TOWER

The name of the LORD is a strong tower; the righteous runs into it and is safe.

—PROVERBS 18:10

Perhaps you are feeling today that living the Christian life is too hard. But I have news for you: God has never asked you to live the Christian life on your own. He wants to live it *in* you and *through* you, to do for you what you could never do for yourself. Christ wants to hide you in His strength—Christ your salvation, Christ your satisfaction, Christ your security.

You see, we could strive all our lives to appear as stunning and majestic as this spectacular view of O'Neil Butte? But why—when already the name of the LORD is our strong tower.

Run to him and be safe. Look to Him and be complete. Don't tarry another moment. "Now is the accepted time; behold, now is the day of salvation" (2 Corinthians 6:2).

GRAND CANYON NATIONAL PARK, ARIZONA

AFTER THE *S*TORM

*F*or *Thou hast been a defense for the helpless . . . a refuge from the storm.*

—Isaiah 25:4

It took Tom five years to get this photograph. That's a long time. But do you know how he caught this incredible view? He patiently waited out a storm.

How long have you waited on the Lord for something? Perhaps you've longed to be married. Or you and your spouse have longed for a child. Isaiah 40:31 promises, "But they that wait upon the LORD shall renew their strength; they shall mount up with wings as eagles; they shall run, and not be weary; and they shall walk, and not faint."

God desires to be your defender when you are helpless, your refuge in the storm. "Wait on the LORD: be of good courage, and He shall strengthen thine heart" (Psalm 27:14). Trust. Wait. He will not fail you.

WIND RIVER RANGE, WYOMING

AN ANCHOR OF THE *S*OUL

We may have strong encouragement, we who have fled for refuge in laying hold of the hope set before us. This hope we have as an anchor of the soul.

—HEBREWS 6:18-19

As a young boy growing up in Florida, I was very familiar with undertows, which could easily cause swimmers to drift out to sea. Similarly in the spiritual life, there are winds of circumstance and currents of carnality that can do the same thing.

Robert Robinson, the hymn writer, penned these words that sum up our cry . . . and our tendency: "O to grace how great a debtor, daily I'm constrained to be / Let Thy goodness, like a fetter, bind my wandering heart to Thee / Prone to wander, Lord, I feel it, prone to leave the God I love / Here's my heart, O take and seal it, seal it for Thy courts above."

So let the storm rage, let the waves buffet, let the wind blow. My anchor holds to Jesus Christ, the Rock of my salvation.

OREGON COAST

HEAVEN AND EARTH

Thou hast made the heavens and the earth by Thy great power and by Thine outstretched arm! Nothing is too difficult for Thee.

—JEREMIAH 32:17

 In the beginning God created the heaven and the earth" (Genesis 1:1). The word used for "God" in this verse is *Elohim*, a plural name for God that comes from two root words: *El*, meaning "strength and unlimited power," and *Allah*, meaning "to keep a covenant."

Aren't you glad God is introduced to us this way in the very first verse of the Bible? You could rephrase this verse to say, "In the beginning Elohim, the God with whom nothing is impossible, the God who always keeps His word, the triune God (Father, Son, and Holy Spirit) created for His pleasure, for His praise, and for His people the heaven and the earth."

Are you facing a hopeless situation today? Then praise His name! For nothing is or has ever been too difficult for God!

WHITE SANDS NATIONAL MONUMENT, NEW MEXICO

$\mathscr{S}$TILL WATERS

$\mathscr{T}$*he* L*ORD* *is my Shepherd, I shall not want. He makes me lie down in green pastures;*
He leads me beside still waters.

*—*P*SALM* 2 3 : 1 - 2

Remember the last time you became sick and had to stay in bed for a few days? If you're like most people, you lay there and wondered about the 1,001 things you could be doing. But God was making you rest instead. Perhaps deep down you had lost hope about your future. And with the hurried pace of your life, you may not have thought you could afford to take a day or two to refresh yourself, contemplate your options, and plan for your future. But your Shepherd knew best. He gently removed your urgency and gave your mind a rest. Peace flooded your soul and soon you could think clearly.

   That same sense of calm and assurance can be yours right now. Green pastures. Still waters. Rest and reflection. The Shepherd is still your only security, your serenity, your sufficiency. Will you trust Him today?

WIND RIVER RANGE, WYOMING

SEASONS OF *L*IFE

*A*nd we know that God causes all things to work together for good to those who love God, to those who are called according to His purpose.

—ROMANS 8:28

 What makes this fall scene so unique? It is the profusion of color from every hue in the fall palate, draped behind a lakeside grove of . . . dead trees. Without the contrast, you see, this would be just another autumn photo. Instead, it is a living portrait of Romans 8:28.

All things do indeed work together for good "to those who love God [and] are called according to His purpose." God weaves a tapestry of pain and joy, of heartache and laughter, into a hopeful future for each of us. Just as He promised in Jeremiah 29:11, "I know the plans that I have for you . . . plans for welfare and not for calamity to give you a future and a hope."

Each moment in the seasons of our life stands alone, but from God's perspective each thread of worry and wonder comes together for our good.

NORTHERN VERMONT

PEACE

Peace I leave with you. . . . Let not your heart be troubled, nor let it be fearful.

—JOHN 14:27

As much as people worry today, I believe it is fast becoming the world's most popular indoor sport. After all, we have many reasons to worry. The ignorant fret because they don't know enough. The educated are troubled because they know too much. The poor worry over their lack of money, while the rich are concerned about losing what they have.

Where can you go to exchange your worries for peace? There's only one place—in Jesus Christ. Jesus brings us hope that the world cannot give or take away.

Think about it: How much good has your worrying done for you so far? Why not give it all to Jesus and trust Him to meet the deepest need of your heart? "Let not your heart be troubled," because He has the peace you need.

WIND RIVER RANGE, WYOMING

THE CHURCH IN THE *Wildwood*

For whatever was written in earlier times was written for our instruction, that through perseverance and the encouragement of the Scriptures we might have hope.

—ROMANS 15:4

Perseverance. That was what Tom needed to get this idyllic scene. You see, the fog had leisurely nestled across this valley for what seemed like the entire day. The other photographers had already left, one by one, and Tom was there . . . alone.

He prayed that God would dissipate the fog—for even a single minute! And wouldn't you know it, the fog lifted just long enough for this photograph to be taken, then quickly rolled back in. But Tom had persevered, and God had heard his prayer.

Have you been asking God about something for years and years, yet He doesn't seem to answer? Perhaps you're pleading for someone to be healed, a relationship to be repaired, or a job to be found. Don't give up. God has a word of hope for you. Will you open His Word today and find the answer?

GREAT SMOKY MOUNTAINS NATIONAL PARK, TENNESSEE

NOW WE SEE *DIMLY*

For now we see in a mirror dimly, but then face to face; now I know in part, but then I shall know fully just as I also have been fully known.

—1 CORINTHIANS 13:12

Hymn writer Carrie Breck wrote, "Only faintly now I see Him / With the darkened veil between / But a blessed day is coming / When His glory shall be seen."

I don't mind telling you that the thought of being swept up to meet the great Lover of my soul face-to-face in glory excites me! I will close my eyes one day in this world, and when I open my eyes again, I will be looking into His face. Glory, hallelujah!

First Peter 1:8 echoes my sentiment when it says that this Jesus "whom having not seen, ye love; in whom, though now ye see Him not, yet believing, ye rejoice with joy unspeakable and full of glory." Because of the promise of God's eternal love, we have a hope that cannot be captured in words.

GRAND TETON NATIONAL PARK, WYOMING

THE MOUNTAIN OF THE *Lord*

Come and let us go up to the mountain of the LORD . . .

that He may teach us about His ways and that we may walk in His paths.

—MICAH 4:2

Have you ever felt like you were lost in the wilderness, being led around in circles? It's time for you to come to the mountain of the Lord. It is time for you to sit at His feet. The time has come for you to learn of His ways so you may walk in His pathways of grace.

God has something most wonderful to share with you—perhaps the answer to prayer you've been seeking, a word of wisdom and direction, a person to share your experience with—but it will take a quietness of heart, a humbleness of spirit, and a teachable mind. Are you ready?

He has a pathway of hope for you to walk, and He will guide you along it. His hope springs eternal, and His plans will not disappoint. Let Him teach you about his ways so you may walk in His paths. This is the provision of hope.

WIND RIVER RANGE, WYOMING

THE
PERSON
OF HOPE

Christ is our hope of glory and the glory of our hope.

—ANONYMOUS

I never grow tired of learning *about* Jesus Christ. But what brings me even greater joy is the relationship I am experiencing day after day *with* Jesus Christ.

As believers, you know, we have the hope of Christ living within us. Colossians 1:27 tells us that when we are saved, Christ enters our life and He becomes our hope of glory. We become His purchased possession, partakers of His divine nature—not just a few of us, not just the best of us. Jesus Christ offers Himself as the hope of glory to each and every person who calls upon Him for salvation. That is Good News!

Oh, taste and see that the Lord is good. Trust Him and make heaven your sure destination. Jesus Christ is truly both our hope of glory, and the glory of our hope.

ZION NATIONAL PARK, UTAH

A NEW *Beginning*

If anyone is in Christ, he is a new creation; the old has gone, the new has come!

—2 CORINTHIANS 5:17

Christians are not just nice people; they are new creations! Just like the new day we see dawning through this lone tree, Christians have awakened to a new life in Christ.

No matter what happened the night before Tom took this picture, the morning shows only the signs of being fresh and new. And no matter what has happened in your past, you can have a new life through Jesus Christ. There are no yesterdays in God's calendar of grace; there are only tomorrows.

Isaiah 1:18 promises that "though your sins be as scarlet, they shall be as white as snow; though they be red like crimson, they shall be as wool." Do you want a new beginning? You can have it in a relationship with Jesus Christ.

GREAT SMOKY MOUNTAINS NATIONAL PARK, TENNESSEE

FOLLOW ME

Then Jesus said to His disciples . . . "Follow Me."

—MATTHEW 16:24

Just as this baby bison needs direction from his mother to get through a blinding snowstorm, we too need direction when our lives get a little stormy. But especially when the way is dim like this, one thing is even better than directions: having someone by our side who can show us the way to go.

Jesus said, "My sheep hear My voice, and I know them, and they follow Me" (John 10:27). Do you want to know how to find God when your path becomes cloudy and overcast? The Lord Jesus Christ is your answer, for He not only can tell you *how* to get to God, He *is* the way to God. He said, "I am the Way, the Truth, and the Life: no man cometh unto the Father, but by Me" (John 14:6).

So follow Him. He will show you the way, because indeed He is the Way.

YELLOWSTONE NATIONAL PARK, WYOMING

A TENDER SHOOT

For He grew up before Him like a tender shoot, and like a root out of parched ground. . . . Surely our griefs He Himself bore, and our sorrows He carried.

—ISAIAH 53:2,4

 In the book of Isaiah, we can read beforehand about the coming Savior who would grow into a tender plant from a root in parched ground. As foretold and fulfilled, the great God of glory did not come in a jeweled chariot accompanied by angels and robed in woven looms of light. Instead, the Infinite became an infant—a fragile babe born in an animal stall.

Why would Jesus come in this way? So that He would be the perfect sacrifice. Hebrews 9:28 says, "So Christ was once offered to bear the sins of many; and unto them that look for Him shall He appear the second time without sin unto salvation."

Jesus did not come to bedazzle. He came to save. What greater hope is there than this?

COLORADO PLATEAU

THE 𝓕ULLNESS OF TIME

But when the fullness of the time came, God sent forth His Son . . .
in order that He might redeem [us].

—GALATIANS 4:4-5

Tom's hike up the mountain was not to be in vain. Climbing through a foot of snow, with storm clouds threatening, Tom reached the ridge just in time to see the sun break through the clouds.

God's timing is always perfect. In the fullness of time, the Bible says, God sent His Son to die on the crossbeams of a tree so that our souls would be redeemed. He did not come one second too soon nor one second too late. The timing of the Savior's entrance into the world was all choreographed and prophesied in the Old Testament.

God has a strategic plan to display His glory and to dispense His grace. He knows exactly what He is doing. And for that alone, there is hope. For me. For you.

GREAT SMOKY MOUNTAINS NATIONAL PARK, NORTH CAROLINA

WHITER THAN SNOW

Wash me, and I shall be whiter than snow.

—PSALM 51:7

When Jesus died on the cross, His blood forever washed sinners whiter than snow. Why would God send His Son to do this? Because of His great love for us.

John 3:16-17 says, "For God so loved the world, that He gave His only begotten Son, that whosoever believeth in Him should not perish, but have everlasting life. For God sent not His Son into the world to condemn the world; but that the world through Him might be saved."

Have you been carrying around a load of guilt over something you've done? It's time you set it down. Friend, Jesus wants to forgive you. He wants to have a relationship with you. Will you receive His gift of forgiveness? You can be as pure as the driven snow.

SAN JUAN MOUNTAINS, COLORADO

REFLECTED LIGHT

The LORD is my light and my salvation; whom shall I fear? The LORD is the defense of my life; whom shall I dread?

—PSALM 27:1

You may be tremendously blessed, but for some reason you do not feel blessed. Perhaps this is because you have forgotten the riches of your life and focused instead on your fears.

How do you turn that around? Your turn your gaze away from self and turn it toward your Savior. Soon His light will reflect upon you, and the breath of heaven will breeze back into your soul. First John 4:4 affirms this promise: "Greater is He that is in you, than he that is in the world." God's mighty power and love can melt away your fear.

Just as Psalm 27 begins with the Person of Hope, so it ends with the same assurance: "Wait on the LORD: be of good courage, and He shall strengthen thine heart: wait, I say, on the LORD" (Psalm 27:14).

GRAND CANYON NATIONAL PARK, ARIZONA

A STEADFAST *Hope*

Fix your hope completely on the grace to be brought to you at the revelation of Jesus Christ.

—1 PETER 1:13

The hope of every Christian believer is not in some*thing*; it is in Some*one*, in Jesus Christ. The hymn writer Edward Mote wrote, "My hope is built on nothing less / Than Jesus' blood and righteousness / I dare not trust the sweetest frame / But wholly lean on Jesus' name."

The grace given to us by God through His Son Jesus Christ gives hope that will never fade away. And how do you define this grace? **G**od's **R**iches **A**t **C**hrist's **E**xpense.

No matter how dark the night grows or how strong the winds blow, the glorious, steadfast hope of every child of God is that our salvation has been purchased for all eternity by Jesus Christ. He gave His life so we could be forgiven. This is our steadfast hope.

CANYONLANDS NATIONAL PARK, UTAH

THE THRONE OF GRACE

Let us therefore draw near with confidence to the throne of grace,
that we may receive mercy and may find grace to help in time of need.

—HEBREWS 4:16

 These swirls of sandstone bathed in sunlight remind me of God's throne. What an awesome picture to imagine! But so many people are fearful of approaching God. They forget that Jesus has prepared the way. Hebrews 4:14 declares, "Seeing then that we have a great High Priest, that is passed into the heavens, Jesus the Son of God, let us hold fast our profession."

If you are fearful, don't stay away because you think you're not good enough. No one is good enough. That is why Jesus gave His life. "For He [God] hath made Him [Jesus] to be sin for us, who knew no sin; that we might be made the righteousness of God in Him" (2 Corinthians 5:21). God's invitation says to "Come." Will you come to Him today?

COLORADO PLATEAU

IN THY LIGHT

For with Thee is the fountain of life; in Thy light we see light.

—PSALM 36:9

Sometimes it's the things you *don't* see that make all the difference.

Tom had worked hard to set up this photo, adjusting his perspective, analyzing and re-analyzing his composition. Then slowly, gradually, light began gleaming through a side opening in the canyon. Suddenly, color and texture began igniting the walls. Still water began dancing with life. Even the pond's green vegetation quietly floated into view and began glowing in the light.

Our lives often feel dull and unimaginative, our circumstances routine, our worth muted by spending too much time in the darkness of everyday life. But "in Thy light," the Psalmist wrote, "we see light." When God enters the equation, things look different. Life appears meaningful again. Value is restored. Hope is reborn.

Step back into His light today, and see if your surroundings don't begin to look brighter.

ESCALANTE WILDERNESS AREA, UTAH

IN *S*ILENCE

My soul, wait in silence for God only, for my hope is from Him.

—PSALM 62:5

Silence is golden. I would venture to say, in fact, that it is more than that. Silence is miraculous in today's fast-paced society. But who has time for stillness?

Or shall I put it another way: Who *doesn't* have time for it? We must realize that God is in the silence. Have you ever heard a tree growing? Or a flower budding? Or the sun bursting through the clouds? But who orchestrated this symphony of silence? God did. We must make time to be silent before Him.

For even when things are silent, God has not left. He is still here, and He is still in control. "Let all the earth fear the LORD: let all the inhabitants of the world stand in awe of Him. For He spake, and it was done; He commanded, and it stood fast" (Psalm 33:8-9). Quiet yourself . . . and listen. Hope is calling.

REELFOOT LAKE STATE PARK, TENNESSEE

AN EVERLASTING *Rock*

Trust in the LORD *forever, for in* GOD *the* LORD *we have an everlasting Rock.*

—ISAIAH 26:4

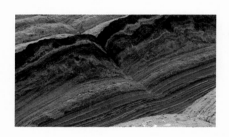

Jesus said, "Whosoever heareth these sayings of Mine, and doeth them, I will liken him unto a wise man, which built his house upon a rock: And the rain descended, and the floods came, and the winds blew, and beat upon that house; and it fell not: for it was founded upon a rock" (Matthew 7:24-25).

Every time you see a rock, it ought to remind you of God's Rock, Jesus Christ—the foundation upon which you can build your life and know that He will always be there for you.

Friend, God loves you. You may tremble on that Rock, but He won't move under you. He will keep you steady. Will you allow the sands of time to wash your life away? Or will you build your life on the Everlasting Rock—Jesus Christ?

COLORADO PLATEAU

LAST LIGHT

And the world is passing away . . .
but the one who does the will of God abides forever.

—1 John 2:17

Perhaps you've known days when you felt yourself in the uncontrollable spin of a windmill blade, a blur of constant motion and activity, yet seemingly going nowhere—caught in the current without meaning or direction. But God has come to give you purpose in the midst of such pointlessness, hope in the face of indifference. He can transform your life into a turbine of His power, redirecting every wave of change into a testimony that will live on for years to come.

This world is passing away, my friend. But there is hope in the person of Jesus Christ—a hope that will endure until the end of time, never fading or faltering, the only light still shining when all others have gone dark. He is your anchor to cling to, your rock to embrace. He is your God, and He is here.

He is the Nature of Hope.

EASTERN COLORADO

PHOTOGRAPHER'S ACKNOWLEDGMENTS

The beauty of nature is such a blessing... a blessing that is doubled when shared with friends. And no project of this magnitude could have been accomplished without the help of friends.

I am so thankful for my pastor, Adrian Rogers, whose godly life has given me such inspiration and instruction. I am honored by your friendship.

The staffs of Love Worth Finding Ministries and Broadman & Holman Publishers once again have been wonderful to work with, especially Julia Flanagan, Ricky King, Lawrence Kimbrough, and Diana Lawrence. Thank you for your dedication to excellence and inspired creativity in editing and designing this book.

My fellow photographers Carl Nilson, Eric Hinson, Mary Hewes, Mike Borum, and Amy Hill have skillfully helped me prepare the photographic manuscript of this book. Thank you. I am a better photographer and better person because of your friendship.

Many others have also participated through their input: Dave Perdue, Sharon Gardner, Barbara Bouton, and Larry Kintner, to name a few. I appreciate your encouragement, counsel, and friendship.

Finally, and most importantly, I am eternally grateful to my Lord and Savior Jesus Christ, who opened my eyes, showed me His beauty, and gave me His friendship.

A wise explorer once said, "In nature man learns to have faith in His Creator." Indeed this is so true, for in nature the art of God can be clearly seen and can speak to the soul and spirit within all of us.

—*Tom Fox*

AUTHOR'S ACKNOWLEDGMENTS

How can I say thank you enough to those who have been such a vital part of this book. At least, I will try.

First and foremost, I want to give God the glory for the nature of hope He has given us through His Son Jesus Christ. The hope we enjoy is clearly displayed in Holy Scripture, and as we see each and every day, it is also reflected in nature. Someone has rightly said, "Books in books, sermons in stone, and God in everything."

Next, I want to say a profound thank you to Tom Fox, who does with a camera what a gifted artist does with palate and brush. Tom has paid a dear price in patience and sometimes discomfort to be at the right place at the right moment to capture on film this feast for our eyes.

Also, I want to thank and recognize Julia Flanagan for her gifted insight and tireless editing to help me put into print these devotional thoughts that express our hope in God. Julia, you are wonderful!

Finally, I want to say thanks to the staffs at Love Worth Finding and Broadman & Holman for their help in making this project all that it is.

—*Adrian Rogers*